A New True Book

RODEOS

By James W. Fain

This "true book" was prepared
under the direction of
Illa Podendorf,
formerly with the Laboratory School,
University of Chicago

CHILDRENS PRESS, CHICAGO

Calf roping, Cheyenne
Frontier Days

PHOTO CREDITS

Carlton C. McAvey—2, 8, 15 (top), 19, 20 (top), 32, 34
(top), 37, 43 (left)
James Fain—4 (2 photos), 6 (2 photos), 10, 11, 23,
25, 26 (top), 29, 34 (bottom), 38, 39 (left), 41
(2 photos), 42, 44, 45
Reinhard Brucker—Cover, 13, 16, 26 (bottom), 39
(right)
James Mejuto—15 (bottom)
Hillstrom Stock Photos—© Thomas Woodrich—12,
18, 20 (2 photos bottom), 24, 31, 43
COVER—Saddle bronc riding

Library of Congress Cataloging in Publication Data

Fain, James W.
  Rodeos.

  (A New true book)
  Includes index.
  Summary: Describes events such as parades, calf
roping, saddle bronc riding, and steer wrestling which
comprise the form of entertainment known as the rodeo.
  1. Rodeos—Juvenile literature. [1. Rodeos]
I. Title.
GV1834.F35 1983   791'.8   82-23460
ISBN 0-516-01685-7   AACR2

TABLE OF CONTENTS

Trick riders and team roping contests are part of a rodeo.

FIRST RODEOS

Rodeos started during the days of cattle drives in the Old West. They were contests among cowboys. They would ride and rope to see who was the best.

Today, millions of people see rodeos each year. Rodeos take place in the United States, Canada, and Australia.

Rodeo parades are
exciting and fun.

6

RODEO PARADES

Most rodeos start with the grand entry. Look at all the colorful cowboys and cowgirls. Look at the beautiful horses.

The announcer greets the people at the rodeo. When the national anthem is played, everybody stands. Cowboys take off their hats to pay respect to their flag. Some people bow their heads in prayer.

A bronc, or bronco, is an unbroken or imperfectly broken horse.

BAREBACK RIDING

Now the cowboys, the cowgirls, the clowns, and the guests leave the arena. It is time for the first event, or contest, bareback bronc riding.

The horses, called broncs, are waiting. Suddenly a chute gate is jerked open. A bronc lunges into the arena bucking and leaping high in the air.

The rider hangs on
tightly. He holds on to a
leather rigging with one
hand. He holds his other
hand high in the air. The
rider jerks his knees and
uses his spurs.

The cowboy must stay
on his horse for eight
seconds to be scored by
the judges. The cowboy
with the highest score
wins.

The eight-second horn sounds. Two men on horseback help the rider get off the bucking bronc. Pickup men work in the saddle bronc riding event, too.

Not every rider can stay on his bronc for eight seconds.

CALF ROPING

Calf roping is next. With a bang the roping chute flies open.

A bellowing calf races into the arena. A cowboy on a fast horse is close behind.

The cowboy swings a rope. He throws a neat loop around the calf's neck. At the rider's signal, the horse stops.

The cowboy jumps off his horse. He runs to the calf and throws it to the ground. Then he ties three of the calf's legs together. When he throws his hands into the air, the judge drops his flag. The cowboy's time is recorded.

While his horse keeps the rope tight, the cowboy throws the calf to the ground. Three of the calf's legs are tied together with a short rope called a piggin' string.

The clock is stopped when the cowboy throws his hands into the air.

This cowboy made a fast run. His time is ten seconds flat.

The winner of the calf roping contest is the person who roped and tied his calf in the fastest time. Fast times are between eight and twelve seconds.

SADDLE BRONC RIDING

Back at the bucking chutes, it is time for saddle bronc riding. The broncs are snorting and pawing at the dirt. None of these horses has been broken. Not one has been trained to carry a saddle or a rider.

Now a saddle has been put on a bronc's back. A leather halter is on its head. A rough braided rein is tied to the halter.

The rider eases down
into the saddle. He picks
up the rein. The bronc
leans into the gate.

Bang! The gate flies
open. A roar comes from
the crowd. The bronc
dashes into the arena. It
bucks and kicks. The
horse tries to buck the
rider off. The rider does

The people who take part in rodeos
are athletes. But even well-trained
athletes can get hurt (right).

his best to stay in the saddle. With a powerful leap the bronc dives to the left. Whoops! The rider keeps going to the right. He lands in a heap in the dusty arena.

No score for this rider. To score points the rider must stay on the horse. Some contests last eight seconds. Others last ten seconds.

STEER WRESTLING

The next event is steer wrestling, or bulldogging. Steer wrestling is fast and wild. Two cowboys on their horses are ready.

One nods his head. At this signal, a longhorn steer bursts from the chute. The two cowboys chase the steer.

A steer breaks out of the chute. The rider on the left is the hazer.
The one on the right is the dogger.

23

One cowboy, the hazer,
keeps the steer running
straight. The other cowboy,
the dogger, slides from his
horse onto the steer's
back. He then grabs the
steer by its horns.

He digs his heels into
the dirt. It takes all his
strength to pull the steer
around. He reaches for the
steer's nose and pulls
back. The steer falls to the
ground. Fast times can be
from three to six seconds.

BARREL RACING

Now it is time for barrel racing, a cowgirl event.

Brightly dressed riders take their turn. They race well-trained horses around the barrels. The barrels are set to look like a clover leaf. The rider who takes her horse through the course the fastest is the winner.

TEAM ROPING

Back at the roping chute, the cowboys are ready for team roping. Two cowboys work together.

One is the header. He ropes the steer around the horns. The other is the heeler. He ropes the steer's hind feet. Both make their catch. When the ropers turn their horses to face each other, the judge drops his flag. It is a fast nine-second run.

The heeler (left) and the header (right) chase their steer.

WILD HORSE RACE

After team roping the cowboys are ready for the wild horse race. Three cowboys will work as a team in this event. They are a mugger, an anchor man, and a rider.

The anchor man holds on to a long rope. The rope is tied to the halter on one of the wild horses.

Horses are turned loose. The anchor man and

Three cowboys take part in the wild horse race.

mugger stop one horse.
They try to hold the horse
in place so the rider can
saddle it. The horse is
kicking and rearing. Finally
the rider cinches the
saddle tight. He jumps on
and rides for the finish line.

A bull rider can only use one hand to hold on to the rope.

BULL RIDING

Bull riding, the most dangerous event, is next. In order to score points, the rider must stay on the bull for eight seconds.

The bull rider looks small. The bull looks very large and mean. The bull weighs from 1,300 to 2,000 pounds.

A rope is all the rider has to hold on to. The rope is called a bull rope. It goes around the bull's body just behind the front legs. This rope is pulled tight on the rider's hand. Only a strong hand will keep the rope in place.

In front of the chutes the rodeo clowns are ready. They are there to protect the rider from the bull.

When the bull rider has a good hold on the bull rope he nods his head. The chute gate opens. The bull explodes into the arena. He kicks high in the air with his hind feet. He spins in a circle.

Suddenly the rider loses his seat. Down he comes. The bull turns to charge. Will the clowns be in

time? Yes, the clowns run
in front of the bull. The
rider runs to safety.
    Even if a rider stays on
for eight seconds he still
has to get off the bull and
make it to safety. Again

the "rodeo lifesavers," the
clowns, rush in and get
the bull's attention. This
lets the bull rider dash to
safety.

RODEO CLOWNS

The clowns look and act silly, but they are very important. They actually put themselves in danger to protect a bull rider.

Clowns act funny, but they have a very important job in the rodeo.

Sometimes a clown will run between the animal and a fallen rider. Sometimes when the rider's hand becomes trapped in the rope the clown will crawl onto the back of the bull in an attempt to free the rider's hand.

The greatest danger to the clowns and riders is not the bull's horns. It is his feet. Getting stepped on has resulted in far more serious injuries than getting hit by the horns.

RODEO PEOPLE

The people who work in rodeos are athletes. They are independent and proud.

A cowboy checks his saddle before an event.

Some people take part
in rodeos and win prize
money. Others just enter
the contests for the prize
ribbons or trophies. No
matter. Everybody wants to
do the best they can.

A rodeo is exciting and fun. It is a piece of living history recalling for millions the days of the Old West.

The heeler ropes a steer's back legs in the team steer roping event.

WORDS YOU SHOULD KNOW

anchor man(ANK • er MAN) —the person in a rodeo who holds the rope tied to a halter on a horse's head

arena(ah • REEN • ah) —an enclosed place where a rodeo is held

athlete(ATH • leet) —a person who is trained for and takes part in sports

bellow(BELL • oh) —a loud roaring noise made by a person or other animals

bronc(BRONK) —a name for a wild or partly trained horse

bulldogging(BULL • dog • ing) —an event in a rodeo where a person tries to wrestle a steer to the ground

chute(SHOOT) —a small, enclosed space just outside a rodeo arena where animals are kept.

cinch(SINCH) —a strong tie used to hold a saddle on a horse

hazer(HAY • zer) —the person in the rodeo who keeps the steer running straight in the bull-dogging event

heeler(HEEL • er) —the person in the rodeo who ropes the steer's hind legs in the team roping event

independent(in • dih • PEN • dint) —not to depend on others

lunge(LUNJ) —a sudden, forward movement

mugger(MUG • er) —the person in the rodeo who ropes a wild horse

qualify(KWAL • ih • fy) —to show your skill in a sports event by fulfilling the basic requirement

rear(REER) —to rise on the hind legs

reins(RAINZ) —long leather straps attached to a horse's head and used by the rider to control the horse

rigging(RIG • ing) —a leather strap attached to a horse's head and held by the rider

rodeo(ROH • dee • oh) — a show where people display their skills in events

spurs(SPERZ) — a metal piece in the shape of a small wheel with spikes that is worn on the heel of a person's boot and used to poke a horse

steer wrestling(STEER RESS • ling) — a rodeo event where a person tries to bring a steer down on its side

trophy(TROH • fee) — a prize that is given to someone who does well

INDEX

About the Author

James W. Fain received his master's degree in Fine Art (Scenic Photography) from Utah State University. He is a free-lance photographer whose specialty is rodeo and scenic photographs. A member of the Rodeo Media Association and the Professional Rodeo Cowboys Association, James Fain has had his photographs and articles published in a wide variety of publications including Western Horseman Magazine, Rodeo Magazine, Horse and Rider, Rodeo Sports News, National Parks Magazine, Westways and Arizona Highways. An expert on rodeos, Mr. Fain also competed in the bareback riding, bull riding, and steer wrestling events in college and professional rodeos. This is the first book he has written for Childrens Press.